JUST TWENTY STOCKS AND A PLAN

CONCENTRATED INVESTING WITH STOCKS & OPTIONS

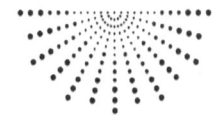

ALAN KERRMAN

NOTABLE MEDIA

Copyright © 2017 by Alan Kerrman, Notable Media.

All rights reserved. No part of this book may be reproduced in any form or by any electronic or mechanical means, including information storage and retrieval systems, without written permission from the author, except for the use of brief quotations in a book review.

The content provided here is for informational purposes only. It should not be considered legal, business, or financial advice. You should consult with an attorney or other professional to determine what may be best for your individual needs.

LEGAL DISCLAIMER: We do not make any guarantee or other promise as to any results that may be obtained from using our content. No one should make any business or investment decision without first consulting his or her own financial advisor and conducting his or her own research and due diligence. To the maximum extent permitted by law, Notable Media and the author disclaims any and all liability in the event any information, commentary, analysis, opinions, advice and/or recommendations prove to be inaccurate, incomplete or unreliable, or result in any investment, business, or other losses. Do your own homework!

Thank you for reading this book. Please consider leaving a review wherever you found this book!

Published by Notable Media • First edition, Version 1.0
ISBN-13: 978-1981951833
ISBN-10: 1981951830

DEDICATION

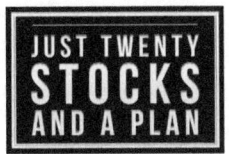

For my wonderful wife and daughter

CONTENTS

Preface vii

Chapter 1   1
Chapter 2   6
Chapter 3   14
Chapter 4   19
Chapter 5   26
Chapter 6   32
Chapter 7   43
Chapter 8   52

About the Author   65
Also by Alan Kerrman   67
Author's Note   69
Index   73

PREFACE

From the author of "Investing with DRIPs," here is a personal finance title for individual investors by an individual investor. This short book takes a quick look at a strategy suggested by Warren Buffett in his famous 20-stock punch card quote which is an intriguing balance of investment ideas and overall discipline. This book includes real-world examples of recent trades, and a general approach to wealth-building, income investing, and retirement planning using a concentrated approach to investing in stocks and strategic options.

CHAPTER ONE

WHY I WROTE THIS BOOK

Thank you for checking out my latest personal finance project. I love this stuff and I'm happy to share this with you (and yours), and I hope it adds to your long-term wealth in some tremendous ways.

Let me first tell you that I am not a financial advisor or registered investment advisor of any kind, and other than my own family's assets, I do not manage anyone else's investments.

Everything included in this book about money, investing, retirement, wealth creation, and more is my opinion (based on reading, experience, and more) and is contains the hard-won knowledge of an individual investor (me!) who wants to share what I've learned with another individual investor (you!).

Knowing that, none of the information here should be considered investment advice in any way, and you always need to consult with your own professional, financial, legal, and tax advisors before you risk any of your hard-earned money on any investment. And even then, I think it's also a very good rule of thumb to never invest a penny in something you don't entirely understand.

(A quick aside: That's why, when I started this book, I hadn't put any of my investing assets into Bitcoin, Ethereum, or one of the other hundreds of available cryptocurrencies because I didn't honestly understand the nature of that technology (the 'blockchain'), the trading risks, and the differences among the 'assets.' But like everything else, I continue doing my homework. Don't worry, this isn't a book about bitcoin. I can gladly say I've made money "testing the waters" on both Bitcoin and Ethereum, but I can't really classify them as investments, but more as trades or speculations. As of this writing, I am not holding any cryptocurrency assets. I will also say that a "currency" that is so volatile that you'd never want to spend it on a consumable item is problematic. My friends in crypto trades tell me that everyone in the near future will buy their pizzas with BTC, but if the price moves wildly, who wants to be the person who spent $500 on a pizza last summer just because you paid with bitcoin? We'll see. It's definitely interesting to watch and read about the debates between *growth* or *bubble*!)

WRITING ABOUT FINANCE

I'm here because I wrote a couple of short personal finances books in the past couple of years: ***Investing in DRIPs***, about dividend investing, and ***Trading Options on Technology Stocks***, with some of my favorite options strategies. I'm sharing what I'm doing with our finances and what I'm learning. I also work full-time in higher education (for now), and run a small online media company. As I said, I'm not a finance professional at all. And I'm quite happy about that.

Why?

I can tell you that with all of my passions, interests, reading, research, and listening to financial podcasts, watching investing videos, and other content, I know from recent discussions that I know more about this stuff than my CPA (sorry, it's true!), or the regional retirement advisor who called me about my university's retirement assets. I don't blame these people for their lack of breadth. They will never be as passionate about my investments as I am. And many professionals are very competent "in their lane," but never had a reason to learn the full scope of what's available in finance.

That said, I think we're in an information and educational boom for individual investors. You can learn so much from the content that's available, which is why I applaud you for reading this and continuing your own financial education.

Most people don't take money seriously, and wonder why they have a poor financial future when they get there. As I've always said to friends and family, it bewilders me how much time most people will spend researching a large purchase (their home, car, furniture, major electronics, etc) or planning a vacation or cruise, but these same people can't be bothered to learn about the growing assets in their retirement accounts or ways to build their family's wealth. But you (and I) are those who will benefit from this interest and passion and desire to continue to learn.

So let's get started.

CHAPTER TWO

INSPIRATION FROM BUFFETT

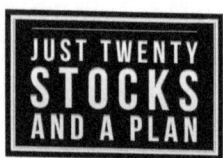

"I always tell the students in business school they'd be better off when they got out of business school to have a punch card with 20 punches on it. And every time they made an investment decision they used up one of those punches, because they aren't going to get 20 great ideas in their lifetime. They're going to get five, or three, or seven and you can get rich off five, or three, or seven. But what you can't get rich doing is trying to get one every day."

— WARREN BUFFETT

JUST TWENTY STOCKS AND A PLAN

I've always been intrigued by the thought of a concentrated portfolio. Part of this is that many of us have good ideas for long-term investments and when it comes right down to it we just didn't hold enough of it to truly make a difference.

I can think of a couple people I know right now who have leveraged large positions in single stocks, along with other broad holdings, as the basis for their wealth, security, and income. One who has been slowly amassing a sizable position in Apple [ticker symbol: AAPL] even before they started paying a regular dividend. The other American friend has a massive holding in Wells Fargo [ticker symbol: WFC] that has allowed him to live a comfortable life overseas and travel for decades.

I started this project because I think that there is incredible wisdom embedded in the Buffett quote and it has been guiding me for years. It's may not be 100% original, even on Buffett's part, but it touches on a few things that go against the grain with traditional investing. This profound advice brings up *discipline, financial mistakes, non-diversification benefits*, *patience*, and so much more. Let's unpack some of these ideas.

FINANCIAL DISCIPLINE

The twenty stock punch card idea implies a level of financial discipline that makes individual research necessary. If you only have a limited number of slots, over time you'd definitely become much more deliberate about your choices. But you'd also get to know the companies very well.

With twenty holdings, you'd be more likely to read each annual report, listen to the earnings calls, and really study the financial metrics of each company. You would consider a company's financial health in the short-term and consider its long-term growth prospects. Reading and following the company, sector, and industry, you would literally become an expert on the assets you were holding.

MAKING MISTAKES WITH MONEY

The next aspect of Buffett's quote which is interesting is the mistakes traders and investors make.

His plan assumes you won't have too many great ideas of your wealth-building lifetime, but with the limited slots available, you'd be more apt to be more deliberate with each choice. And because of the concentrated nature of your final list, you'd have enough of your winners to offset any choices that shouldn't have been in your top twenty.

NON-DIVERSIFICATION

This leads us to the concept of *non-diversification*. Twenty stocks might sound very concentrated to some investors who own literally hundreds of assets over their lifetime. The problem is that, especially in mutual funds, wide diversification like this is essentially an index fund but without the low fees. If you want "exposure" to every asset class — hands off — then index funds make sense, but once you have too many holdings, even winners can't help your long-term growth very much.

We are often told that diversification improves performance, reduces risk, and sets us up for broad-based gains. But the truth is most diversification comes with a price. (This is the argument for index funds. And I really think it still is a pretty solid choice for anyone who doesn't want to take the time to understand how the market works. For those investors too busy with work, family, relationships, or just living their lives, an S&P500 index fund [ticker symbol: SPY] with the lowest possible fees is probably the best bet.

Since I work in higher education, my retirement assets are in a 403b account, so I'm not allowed to trade individual stocks, options, or futures with those assets, even though it's my money. So in that account, all my contributions and my small employer match are going into domestic and international index funds until I get control of that money myself.

Even if you're able to choose a mutual fund with a well-respected manager with a solid track record who has created a decent growth, value, or blend fund with a wide array of holdings, you're just moving closer to index investing — but with one significant difference. You're overpaying in fees.

THE POWER OF PATIENCE

The next benefit here is patience. Once you decide to purchase a holding, especially something you fully believe in, you're now willing to accumulate a position in that stock over time, building it into a larger and more substantial asset. But this isn't the old-fashioned *buy and hold* strategy. It's about long-term strategic wealth building.

> *"If you aren't willing to own a stock for ten years, don't even think about owning it for 10 minutes."*
>
> — WARREN BUFFETT

Your twenty stock choices are not trades, they are long-term concentrated investments. Work the strategies to maximize cash-flow and reduce costs, but whenever possible, leave them alone.

How? Let's take a look.

COST BASIS REDUCTION VS. DOLLAR COST AVERAGING

The basis for this strategy is to work now for long-term accumulation of the twenty holdings (or assets) while continually reducing the cost of those assets with a series of options, dividend, and hedging strategies. In a perfect world, these stocks continue to pay you even after they've become become paid for ("with the house's money," as they say in Las Vegas, although I'm not much of a gambler).

One thing I've spent a lot of time thinking about and researching lately is how cost basis reduction (CBR) should not be equated to dollar-cost-averaging (DCA). Dollar cost averaging is powerful in that as you make purchases over a long period of time, you get a variety of entries that helps average out your entries, but many trader/investors make the mistake of thinking that doubling down after overpaying is simply DCA. It's not, and it's often a very costly mistake. Dollar cost averaging is best when it is a regular occurrence with the same investing amount, for example monthly buys of $500 or $1000 of a stock. Cost basis reduction is the process by which you track the actual overall net cost of your investments as they go lower based on money received (i.e., options premiums, dividends).

To do this, you have to be willing to enter and exit your twenty holdings as necessary to build wealth. You're not 'day trading' or 'swing trading' these stocks, but you're impacting CBR by being willing to go to all cash with a particular stock. We'll discuss this concept more later.

The goal is a portfolio of holdings that can either be sold off for gains, or mined for dividend and option premium income when you need retirement income — or both.

CHAPTER THREE

BIG BOSS OWNER

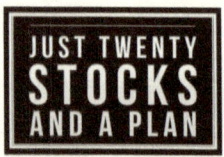

Let's continue into the heart of the strategy and the ideas behind this concentrated approach.

The hardest part is coming up with your punch card selections. You need to choose twenty stocks (companies) that you really can see yourself owning over an extended period of time.

For me (and my wife), it changes a fair amount of the time as we reconsider our investing landscape. But imagine this: Since you're investing for yourself (and your retirement) that means depending on growth and value over decades. (Even if you're retiring this year, you need your assets to grow for your life expectancy and then beyond to possibly leave behind for your loved ones, charitable giving, and more.)

I always imagine my twenty holdings as benefitting my wife and I now, and becoming great assets for our daughter to hold throughout her life, and for the benefit of her future family. (It's a crazy thought for me right now!)

BRAINSTORMING SOME STOCKS

So do I believe that Apple [ticker symbol: AAPL] will be an important company decades from now, or perhaps Tesla [ticker symbol: TSLA] or maybe Amazon [ticker symbol: AMZN]? Maybe I believe that American Express [ticker symbol: AXP] is a timeless brand or perhaps that Wells Fargo & Company [ticker symbol: WFC] will last for another hundred years. There are five ideas right there, but you get the concept. This part is up to you.

It's useful to invest in companies, products, or services you know, use, and understand, and then research their business and basic valuations.

(Much can be found online about ways to look at earnings ratios, free cash flow, and more.)

But I believe the best way to approach this purchase is to imagine that you are a multi-billionaire — yes, stay with me for a second — and that you are writing a check today and buying the entire company.

If you bought the whole company — not just a few shares — would you buy it?

Using this 'mind experiment' can imagine you being the **BIG BOSS OWNER** of Wells Fargo and Company (ticker symbol: WFC), Disney [ticker symbol: DIS], or Walmart (ticker symbol: WMT). Picture which companies — which assets — that you would be happy to own for the next ten, twenty, thirty years of your life. Which companies could you imagine delivering you and your family growth, income, or value over your lifetime?

It's hard because you must also imagine what companies that you think will still be profitable, growing, or even in existence in twenty or thirty years. (If you have kids, or grandkids, imagine giving them the entire company — you can do that because you're still a 'billionaire' — and consider whether that company might still be significant, relevant, and successful when they are adults with children and grandchildren of their own.

What companies would you buy if you could own the entire thing?

WE LIKE APPLE & ALPHABET

Let me continue with a couple of our examples. We could imagine owning Apple (ticker symbol: AAPL) forever. It is one of our twenty.

Why?

Because not only is it a respected brand with important products and technologies in many people's lives, but we think it has enough cash holdings for all sorts of future research, growth projects, or talent or technology acquisitions.

We also feel similar things about Alphabet [ticker symbol: GOOGL] because of their wide-reaching technologies and infrastructure. It's also possible that all internet, web, and mobile (information) searches will just follow whatever technology is current as our society develops (audio, 3D, virtual reality, etc.) and that they will continue to remain relevant. It is another long-term holding for us.

On the flip side, I believe retail companies like Sears and K-Mart, both part of Sears Holdings [ticker symbol: SHLD], and internet former-giant Yahoo [ticker symbol: YHOO] won't exist in ten years. (Maybe even Twitter [ticker symbol: TWTR]!)

I think components of those companies will likely be broken up and sold off to other companies and the underlying value of those current stocks will completely disappear. It's only my opinion, but it's based on what I've been seeing with malls closing (the "retail apocalypse" as some call it), and various publicly-reported management decisions.

Of course, even with companies I admire there are risks, so let discuss those next.

CHAPTER FOUR

LET'S TALK ABOUT RISK

As an individual investor, I've grown to understand risk in ways I couldn't imagine even five years ago. There are levels to risk, and many individual investors overemphasize some of these to the point that they completely undercut growth and then ignore others.

First a quick story...

I was talking to my stubborn — but wonderful — older sister here who is so lifelong suspicious of Wall Street and investing that all of her retirement assets — inside her tax-deferred accounts — were in money-market funds for a very long time. Money market!

When I made the argument that she was wasting valuable time for growth and compounding, and that her real risk wasn't about losing her hard-earned money, but that inflation would mean that her super-safe money would be far less potent for her future needs, she relented a little.

Over time, I helped her see that it was a combination of inflation risk, opportunity cost, and all-or-nothing thinking that was her biggest danger. (She's on track now, but still mad that I was right, as siblings often are)

RISK MANAGEMENT

Understanding risks in the market can help you choose a wide array of holdings for your twenty investments:

So let's talk about that risk:

- There is always **market risk**. If we enter a market downturn or pullback, or even a full-scale bear market, nearly all stocks will come down. The number is generally that 75% of all stocks move with the market direction.

- There is **geographical risk**. Assume there is a drought, war, political strife, recession, or some other event in a specific country or region. Any assets associated with that place — companies headquartered there or that regularly do business in those markets — are suddenly riskier by extension.

- There is **sector/industry risk**. Think of the recent drop in oil prices and how that profit margin compression affected nearly every company in the energy and energy services sector.

- There is **individual company risk**. Things like bankruptcy, scandals, mismanagement, or even product failures and recalls can affect a stock price. Think of the recent safety issues of those smartphone fires with the 70-year old Korean corporation Samsung [ticker symbol: SSNLF].

Market risk and individual company risk is hard to avoid, so we don't. Geographical risk can be mitigated by choosing companies that sell their products or services broadly or that aren't too tied to a single region, country, or economy. Sector/industry risk can be controlled by varying your exposure in your twenty stocks.

Even if you believe in only technology companies, you might choose the best of breed and choose something in another sector for protection.

TWENTY STOCKS MEANS A 5% TARGET

But the risk in a concentrated portfolio of 20 holdings is not as simple as it seems. With $50,000 to invest, twenty holdings would assume that each asset is valued at 5% of the total or $2500. In reality, it could also be as close to that number which helps get to 100 share trading blocks (for options).

Even if you only have $2500 to invest, you might decide to invest in only two of your underlying ideas this year, but as you add assets later you can add diversification later.

For investors with $100,000 to invest for example, twenty holdings means assets that are, on average, about $5000 each. If your goal portfolio is $1,000,000 in assets, that makes each holding approximately $50,000 in value.

But with our previous example, as you continue to add investment assets over your working lifetime, it's possible to start off more concentrated in your early years.

AN EXAMPLE USING AMERICAN EXPRESS

Let's go through one scenario. Assume that one of your twenty great investment ideas is to buy American Express stock for the long-term. (We're customers of AXP, but haven't decided yet on whether it's on our list!)

One hundred shares of American Express [ticker symbol: AXP] at a recent price of $98.90 would cost about $9890. Those hundred shares would generate a 1.43% dividend yield and open up the possibility of selling puts and calls to enter or exit the position.

For those worried that this purchase is more than $5000 as outlined above, remember that as you add more assets and reduce your cost basis with dividends and premiums, your AXP position would become a smaller proportion of your overall portfolio.

Using recent prices, I could enter a 100-share position in American Express, four months out, by selling a cash-secured put at the $95 strike for about $310 dollars, minus fees. If I get exercised on this put, I'll own 100 AXP shares at $9500 minus the premium received ($310), or about $9190, or $91.90 per share. Then I'll start collecting dividends and selling upside calls to lower my risk, lower my cost basis, and amplify the dividend yield.

(Remember selling a put obligates us to buy at a certain strike price and selling a call obligates us to sell at a given strike price, up until expiration of the option.)

Each quarter, I would try to sell an upside call at a higher strike price at a date on the calendar beyond the upcoming dividend payout date. The goal is to collect dividends and premiums that lowers the outlay of my initial investment. Over time, the plan is to return all my initial investment capital, but still hold the stock. Then I can build another position in another company.

In this example, if AXP stays above $95, I'll keep the $310 premium (minus fees) and start my 20-stock card with an American Express gain, even though I don't own the stock yet.

In the coming chapters, we'll look at a real world example of this in one of our rollover retirement accounts with the big box store Target [ticker symbol: TGT].

CHAPTER FIVE

CONCENTRATED INVESTING

As I mentioned before, in a perfect world, my twenty stock portfolio would be a nice mix of solid, stable dividend-paying stocks, growth stocks, and legacy brands that will all still be flourishing in twenty or thirty years.

The perfect way to build this portfolio over time is get paid to buy stocks through a combination of selling puts and put spreads. Also, once the positions are started you'll received dividend payouts, and selling upside calls against your holdings as well as some additional puts and call spreads depending on market conditions.

What this means is that over time each position will have a rotating but slowly accumulating share count, but at times could be out of the position completely and back all in cash.

SELLING PUTS TO OPEN YOUR POSITIONS

What this also means is that it's possible to sell puts for quite a while in one of your twenty stock ideas (like the AXP example above) and have the stock continue to stay above your obligated buy price (your put option's strike price) and generate a positive cash flow for you in a stock that you don't even own yet.

Then if you choose to buy the stock outright on a down market day, or during a pullback, the cash you've already received by selling put premiums to initiate the position would reduce your cost basis.

For example, imagine that you've chosen the Walt Disney Company [ticker symbol: DIS] as one of your twenty ideas. (Another maybe for us, by the way!)

With the stock recently trading around $110.32, you could sell $110 put options three months out for a recent bid of $430 (minus fees). Assume you did that a couple times over several months and Disney stayed above $110, so you kept almost $850 in options premiums, but you still don't own any DIS stock.

On a down day after the second put expires in your favor, imagine that you decide to purchase the stock outright for $108.49, paying $10,849 for 100 shares. Your adjusted cost basis is actually the $10849 minus the approximate $850 in put premiums (two cycles), or $9999, or $99.99 per share.

As you collect the semiannual dividend of $0.78 per share ($1.56 per year or 1.48% yield), you'll reduce your basis by even more if you take back the cash, or expand your holdings if you reinvest your dividends (which is better for compounding.)

WHY PUT SPREADS INSTEAD OF CASH-SECURED PUTS?

Sometimes you know a stock might move down, so you expect that it will come down to your put price, or that it may drop faster than you are comfortable.

Let me explain.

Let's continue with our example with Disney, at a moment when the stock was trading at $110.57.

If you sold a $105 cash-secured put for two-months out on Disney stock, you could take in about $189 (minus transaction fees.)

Since that strike price ($105) is 5.03% lower than the current price ($110.57) of the stock, you have a built-in buffer for your purchase. If the stock goes higher, you keep the put premium $189. If the stock stays flat, you also can keep the put premium. And if the stock falls, but no more than 5.03%, then you can keep that premium as well.

Imagine this as your opening move toward building a position in Disney, if the put expired worthless — in your favor — you could begin your Disney tracking with a gain of say $180.26, for example. ($189.00 premium minus an estimated $7.99 transaction fee minus an estimated $0.75 per option contract fee.)

But with a put spread, instead of a cash-secured put in place as your mechanism for entering the stock, you'll have a long protective put below your short put to protect you against a falling market, and also something that can go up in value as Disney moves towards your strike price.

So instead of selling only a $105 put (cash secured, or on margin), you would simultaneously sell this $105 put and buy the $100 strike put below for protection. This would limit your upside and downside, and give you an additional gain if the DIS stock falls and you still want to let the $105 put get exercised. You'll start your position, and you'll be able to sell the protective put for hopefully more than you paid for it, depending on the move.

HERE ARE THE SPECIFICS

In this example the $105 put you sell (for $189) and the $100 put you buy (at $94), would net you $95, and limit your risk to the downside. As DIS fell toward $105, the $100 put should increase in value of there is time left on the contract. You would re-sell the $100 put for a small gain and allow the $105 put to be exercised.

With this trade you would enter the DIS position at $105 or $10,500 for 100 shares minus the $189 and whatever you made on the $100 put. (It's possible to buy it at $94 and sell at $125, a gain of $31 for example, and add that to your income to offset the purchase.) $10500 - $189 (105 put) - $31 (gain on 100 put) = $10280 or $102.80 per share.

The power of this strategy is amplified with multiple holdings at various points on the cycle. Tracking your basis over time with a simple ledger or spreadsheet is what makes this process fun, clear, simple, and rewarding.

So let's take a look at that in the next chapter.

CHAPTER SIX

THE BIG PICTURE FIRST

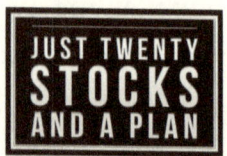

One of the first things you need to do is total all of your own long-term assets as a group, even if they're spread across various accounts.

For some this could mean a combination of long-only mutual fund accounts, if you have those, and any other assets that have limited choices or control. Among the rest of the assets (personal savings, trading accounts, self-directed IRAs, Roth accounts, etc.), this is where you can approach your twenty stocks idea.

Because my wife and I — happily married for years and on the same page about our finances — consider all of our resources pooled, we actually have a single twenty stock list between us and a big picture list of accounts. (For the *naysayers* of romance out there, even if I die or we get a divorce, she gets all of this or at least half anyways, so this approach makes sense!)

What follows are the real trade details from a rollover IRA account where my wife and I built a position in Target [ticker symbol: TGT], a big box retail play that is one of our twenty long-term choices.

We both like the store, the approach to retail and grocery, the management, and the dividend. I think they benefit from the mall closings (the so called retail apocalypse) and I think they have some solid defense against online sales. In my region, many people shop for clothes, housewares, and groceries at the centrally located Target store, a process with some advantages over online purchasing (i.e., Amazon [ticker symbol: AMZN]).

ALAN KERRMAN

OUR TARGET TRADES

This section will give you a clear idea of how this entire strategy of concentrated investing works. We chose Target [ticker symbol: TGT] as one of our twenty after we made sure that we had limited retail exposure anywhere else among our holdings, except for a few 403(b) index funds.

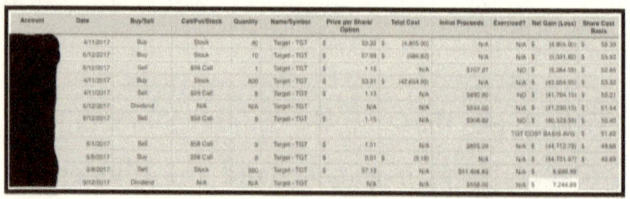

The image is a screenshot from our spreadsheet, but I'll outline the steps here to make the whole process clearer. These trades were made in a rollover IRA account from a previous employer where it's not possible to make additional contributions. The balance was about $47K.

After trading in the 60's in February of 2017, Target's stock was down to the low $50's in April.

- We bought 800 shares of Target at

JUST TWENTY STOCKS AND A PLAN

$53.31 on 04/11/17 and paid $42,654.95.
- We sold eight May '17 calls (covered calls) at the $55 strike for $113 each for a total intake of $890.80, lowering the total cost of the shares to $41,764.15.
- Knowing that Target had a June dividend coming up, we also bought an additional 90 shares at $53.32 for a total cost of $4805.00.
- On May 30, 2017, Target was below $55 so we kept the $890 option premium.
- On June 12, 2017, we received our Target dividend (as cash) of $0.60 per share on 890 shares for a payment of $534.00. This reduced our TGT cost to $41,230.15.

When we started in April 2017, we bought 890 shares and obligated them to be taken away near or around the dividend date. The position brought in over $1420 in premiums and dividends in the first couple months.

Once we had the additional cash in the account

from the expired calls and the dividend, we then bought a little more Target (to round out the option lots) and started the process again.

- We bought 10 more shares of Target on 6/12/17 at $57.99, for a total of $586.82, to bring our holdings to a round 900 shares.
- We then sold 9 contracts of the Jul'17 $59 call options at $115 each, for a total intake of $1014.09. They expired worthless on 7/2817, in our favor, and it continued to reduce our overall cost of the shares.
- Because the stock had moved so far so quickly (7.16%), we sold the 900 shares on 09/08/17 (temporarily) for $57.13 for a gain of $3361.35.
- We had already qualified for the next dividend payment, so on 9/12/17 we received a cash payment of $558.00.

JUST TWENTY STOCKS AND A PLAN

Symbol	Quantity	Opening Transaction Date	Price $	Net Amount $	Type	Closing Transaction Date	Price $	Net Amount $	Realized Gain $	Term
TGT	800	04/11/2017	53.31	42,654.95	S	09/08/2017	57.13	45,696.76	1,041.82	Short
TGT	90	04/11/2017	53.32	4,805.75	S	09/08/2017	57.13	5,140.89	335.14	Short
TGT May 26 '17 $56...	-8	04/11/2017	1.13	-890.80	OX	05/26/2017	0.00	0.00	890.80	Short
TGT	10	06/12/2017	57.9874	586.82	S	09/08/2017	57.13	571.21	-15.61	Short
TGT Jul 28 '17 $59 Call	-8	06/12/2017	1.15	-908.83	OX	07/28/2017	0.00	0.00	908.83	Short
TGT Jul 28 '17 $60 Call	-1	06/12/2017	1.15	-107.27	OX	07/28/2017	0.00	0.00	107.27	Short
TGT Sep 08 '17 $58 Call	-9	08/01/2017	1.01	-895.10	BC	09/08/2017	0.01	-9.18	885.92	Short
Total				$45,247.52				$51,399.68	$6,152.16	

Date	Type	Description (show categories)	Amount ($)
09/11/17	Dividend	TARGET CORP CASH DIV ON 900 SHS REC 08/16/17 PAY 09/10/17	558.00
06/12/17	Dividend	TARGET CORP CASH DIV ON 890 SHS REC 05/17/17 PAY 06/10/17	534.00

At the end of the cycle, we made a combined total of $7244.16 on a combination of stock appreciation, dividends, and option premiums. The biggest win was this was inside a rollover IRA account that was closed to new contributions.

The plan was to sit on cash for another entry and then re-enter Target by selling a CSP (cash-secured put) below the market.

In full transparency, it doesn't always work out this well. In one of our accounts, we started building a position in General Electric [ticker symbol: GE] only to have the stock go very hard against us.

HOW TO SELECT THE OPTIONS TO SELL

I know from conversations with my wife that the trickiest part for her to learn was which options to sell, both for new holdings and also current positions.

If you've ever watched the amazing educational network Tastytrade (online and on Youtube), you'll know that the ideal time for selling options is about 45 days out. That's a good balance between receiving enough premium for the risk and a quick enough time decay. For us, that six week window is a rule of thumb.

The other factor is the volatility of the underlying stock. If the stock has already been falling and is close to its 52-week low, the put premiums you'll receive for selling a cash-secured-put (CSP) might seem pretty good. Same thing with a hot growth stock on an up day. That's a perfect time to sell an upside call that requires more price appreciation for you before the call buyer can take the stock away from you. (Notice the second round of calls in Target above required the stock to move up to

$59 before they could be exercised, a gain of $1 on 900 shares, or $900 plus the $1014 options premium.

HERE ARE SOME MORE EXAMPLES

Let's look at a couple of examples using real stock and option prices quoted online:

If we wanted to open a position in Tesla [ticker symbol: TSLA], this is how we would evaluate the options. The stock recently traded at $305, in the upper middle of a 52-week range of $182 to $389.

One hundred shares of TSLA would cost $30,500 at its current price, but since it's been trending down for a while, selling a put far below the stock price gives some safety. For a December put sale, the February options at the strike price of $270 have a bid listed at $905. This means that someone will pay you $905 today if you promise to buy TSLA at $270 if it's at or below $270 at any point up to Feb, 18, 2018. So of course, if you like TSLA and you think it's a good buy here at $305, then it's an even better deal 11.47% lower at $270 with a $900 bonus.

With the options premium $270 x 100 shares =$27000 minus the premium received $905, your adjusted cost for TSLA would be $26,095 (before fees), or $260.95, over 14% lower than buying the stock right here.

Of course, if you're wrong and you tie up $26K for a couple months and the stock stays here, you get to keep the $905 for your trouble. If you think the stock might really drop, consider the spread idea where you sell the $270, but buy a put below that to protect yourself if it keeps dropping and to offset your costs when you exercise at $270.

In other position, let's say you own shares in AquaAmerica [ticker symbol: WTR], the water utility. It has a dividend yield of about 2.17% with a recent stock price of $37.67. Because it's very close to its 52-week high of $38.20, the options premiums (calls) should be selected both for time value (duration) and dividend capture. When I look on Yahoo Finance, I see that the stock pays dividends in February, May, August, and November.

Ideally, I would like to qualify for the dividend and cover the stock with upside calls. Depending on the timing, it's possible to select a call high enough that even if the stock is exercised away from you, it's worth it to not collect the dividend.

The recent dividend payout on WTR is $0.205 per share, or $20.50 per hundred shares. In December, the calls for March are split at $5 increments, so $30, $35, and $40 with relatively low volume. You could sell the $35 call, collect the difference between the bid/ask spread of about $3, but that's essentially obligating the stock out at what you paid ($35 + 3 = $38.00) If you collect the $20 dividend and the $33 stock appreciation, you'll only make $53 on this, minus fees. But again, think about a concentrated holding of $37K instead of $3700 and the gain is now $530 in the same time frame.

If the long term goal is to build a $1,000,000 dollar portfolio, you might end up with $50K worth of a stock like this which at $37 per share is over 1300 shares. Now the small dividend and premiums start to add up to a bigger pay day. At $0.205 per share, 1300 shares pays $1066 in dividends each year, even before selling any calls. The only danger here is the thin options trading volume. That might make some trades you'd like to do, hard to fill.

OUR OTHER ACCOUNTS

In some of our other accounts - some retirement and some taxable, we have some complete and incomplete trading blocks of shares for our list of twenty.

For example, with Apple trading recently at $169.80, it takes almost $17K to have an optionable block of 100 shares. This account that has Apple, also has Alphabet, which at about $1000 a share requires a $100K to trade options contracts.

Next up, let's discuss some questions about the strategy.

CHAPTER SEVEN

QUESTION & ANSWERS

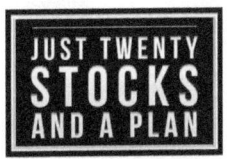

In this chapter, I thought I would try to anticipate some of the questions you might have about this strategy and answer them in one place. Some credit for these questions goes to a few of my friends, relatives, and co-workers who asked such interesting things recently when I told them about this project.

So let's dive right into the list:

> *Q. Do I need to come up with all twenty stock ideas at once?*
> *A. No, this could develop over a period of a few years or more.*

> *As you can tell from the text, we have some clear ideas of some of our holdings, but many open slots on our idea card.*

Q. Isn't options trading really dangerous?

A. In this strategy, holding the stock alone is a little more risky. If you're selling options for premium, the money you take in lowers your overall outlay of funds and your risk.

Q. Can this strategy be a blend of stocks, mutual funds, and ETFs?

A. Ideally, it can be twenty of anything because the strategy limits the holdings to 5% of your total investments, so if one of your choices was index fund and one was cryptocurrency, that's fine, although the hedging (options) and dividend aspects are different, or non-existent.

Q. Can I buy one holding now just to get to 100 share block for options?
A. Yes, as long as you keep saving investment funds and put any new capital into a secondary choice.

Q. What about my company's stock options? How does this apply?
A. Stock options given to employees are an example of how non-diversification can make you rich. Imagine a big pile of shares of Facebook or Walmart earned at work. The only caveat is to balance all of your other investing away from your company stock,

> *sector, and industry. Imagine your company going broke or bankrupt (Enron, Bear Stearns) and you lose your job, your stock options portfolio value, and the bulk of your retirement assets (or pension) all at once. Ouch! Be careful!*

Q. *Do you have to choose dividend-paying stocks?*
A. *Not necessarily, but the extra payouts (=profit sharing) helps lower your cost-basis getting you closer to return of all your capital.*

Q. *In the Target example, you didn't reinvest the dividends into fractional shares. Why not?*
A. *Because we can't deposit cash into that account, every dividend payment we receive*

is like making a retirement contribution. The cash from dividends and options premiums gives us more choice, like pivoting to another holding or buying less of the Target and adding another choice from our top twenty list.

Q. Options seem complicated. What strategies do I need to learn?

A. The concepts behind options are simple. In my experience, and since they expire, it always better to be a seller of options rather than a buyer. The only strategies you need to learn are cash-secured puts, covered calls, and put spreads, also called credit spreads, or bull put spreads. The other strategies are not necessary to build this portfolio of long-term wealth.

Q. What happens if I'm trading too? How does this strategy apply?

A. I think of trading as speculation and this wealth-building as investing. Even if you trade, aim to earn money and park it in assets you'd be happy to hold over time. This applies to any short-term gains or strategies (futures, cryptocurrency, other options strategies, swing trading stocks, forex, etc.)

Q. When should you start investing?

A. Save for your 'future self' as soon as you can. Even if you feel like you're starting late, don't let that dictate your decisions.

Q. If you have massive growth in one of your twenty holdings, do you re-balance at the end of the year?

A. No, just add new contributions to other areas in your portfolio. (In retrospect, we say that because we probably would have stayed in the Target position, even though it had moved over 7% in a short amount of time.)

Q. What do you think are the biggest pitfalls of trading and investing, especially for individual investors?

A. The balance of fear and greed are strong. Fear of losing, not understanding what you're doing, or fear of missing out (FOMO) are powerful and should be dealt with slowly and carefully. Greed also makes people make very bad choices. Don't be afraid to step back, take your profits, and go to cash. Waiting on the sidelines with ready capital is a powerful place to be, especially when a pullback occurs.

Q. What happens when one of the dividend stocks cuts its dividend?
A. You don't necessarily need to sell, but I might stop building that position and wait for the stock to recover. (this happened to us years ago in Supervalu, the grocery stock.)

Q. This process seems time-consuming: choosing stocks, watching for their dividends, then selecting calls or puts to sell. Then multiply that times twenty holdings. Isn't it going to be overwhelming?

A. No. At most it's a couple hours per month because most of the time you're waiting for the dividends to come in or for the options to expire.

CHAPTER EIGHT

FINAL THOUGHTS

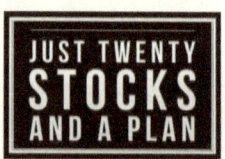

Since the bulk of the work in this strategy is to identify your twenty long-term investments, that's the part that should take the most research, homework, and reading.

Here are a a few ideas on how and where to do that.

1. Make a list of all the companies you trust, products/services you use, and brands you respect. Consider which ones might still be in business in thirty to fifty years from now, and remove those which seem like that might not be evergreen. Start there!
2. Read finance sites like Yahoo Finance, Google Finance, Seeking Alpha, Stocktwits, and elsewhere for ideas of new and established companies and a wide range of industries to research.
3. Look at lists of dividend aristocrats and companies that have returned shareholder value for a record number of years. The ability to distribute and increase dividend payments over a long period of time is a signal of a solid business model.
4. Explore leading mutual funds at Morningstar, Yahoo Finance, and elsewhere to see what the top ten holdings are of some of the most respected funds. For example, looking at the large cap growth mutual fund TRBCX (T. Rowe Price's Blue Chip

Growth Fund), I see that the top ten holdings recently included Amazon [ticker symbol: AMZN], Facebook [ticker symbol: FB], Alphabet [ticker symbol: GOOG], Priceline [ticker symbol: PCLN], Microsoft [ticker symbol: MSFT], Alibaba [ticker symbol: BABA], Visa [ticker symbol: V], Mastercard [ticker symbol: MA], UnitedHealth Group [ticker symbol: UNH], and Boeing [ticker symbol: BA]. By comparison, Fidelity's Blue Chip Growth Fund (FBGRX) includes some of the same holdings but also has Apple [ticker symbol: AAPL], NVIDIA [ticker symbol: NVDA], Tesla [ticker symbol: TSLA], Salesforce [ticker symbol: CRM], Broadcom [ticker symbol: AVGO], and Home Depot [ticker symbol: HD] in its recent top ten holdings.

5. If you search online for stock screeners, you'll be able to sort for stocks by earnings ratios, dividend yield, market capitalization, and whether or not the stocks are optionable. Try screeners

over at Finviz, CNBC, Motley Fool, and others. (The concept of dividend-paying stocks and selling options is the key for me as a hedge. Otherwise, it's just a matter of being long the stock waiting for price appreciation. Then the problem is that you have to liquidate the stock to take advantage of those gains. Full circle, that's why cryptocurrency is just speculation for me at this point and not a viable investment. The choices with Bitcoin or Ethereum are to be long, or sell and be in cash. There is no return of capital (earnings), and until the futures or other derivatives come online, there's no way to hedge by selling premium. I'd gladly cap upside in a cryptocurrency by buying at a high dollar amount and selling an upside call to some growth seeker who think the coins will appreciate another 1000% next year and the year after. I'd be happy to buy BTC at $10K and sell someone a fat call option to buy it from me in six months at $25K or some of the other crazy numbers I've seen. Then at least, I'd have some downside protection if the 'asset' slips. I could at least sell calls. Since I can't, it's very, very dangerous. Same goes for penny stocks, and any stocks with options, or dividends.)

6. If your worried about fees related to buying stocks slowly over time, you can start out in DRIP plans for some stocks. Low monthly purchases direct from the transfer agents with quarterly dividend reinvestments might be the best way to keep costs down. Once you have one hundred shares, or multiples of a hundred you can transfer the shares into a trading account in your name where you can also employ the options strategies included here. Find DRIPs available at Computershare, Wells Fargo Shareowner online, and elsewhere.

7. Take a look at sector lists to make sure you're diversified. If you're in manufacturing or retail, look at energy (traditional, alternative, services, etc.), or if you're leaning towards a lot of

JUST TWENTY STOCKS AND A PLAN

financial or technology stocks, look at health care stocks, or utilities (gas, electric, wind, water, etc.) But do your research and be patient. There are ten broad sectors: consumer discretionary, consumer staples, energy, financial, healthcare, industrials information technology, materials, real estate, telecommunications services, and utilities. Inside of that there are sixty-eight industries with companies ranging from automobiles to beverages, chemicals, software, media, to hotels, and everything in between.

It takes making of habit of investing to accumulate a large enough holding in a position to be impactful. It also takes discipline to not trade around from company to company.

That's the power of Buffett's advice. In his own Berkshire Hathaway [ticker symbol: BRK.A] he has been holding and accumulating stock in Coca-Cola [ticker symbol: KO] for more than twenty-five years.

Because of that, they hold more than 400 million shares, worth more than $16 billion dollars and receive over $500 million in dividends each year. It's an over 9% stake in the company.

And interestingly, he first added the KO stock to his holdings after the 1987 stock market crash buying a billion dollars worth or so at a time when the prices were very low. Trading recently at about $46, Coca-Cola has a 3.25% dividend yield. It's an interesting company with over twenty brands including Coca-Cola, Powerade, Dasani, Nestea (joint venture with Nestlé), Minute Maid, Sprite, VitaminWater, Fuze, Honest Tea, and more. When you dig down into a company and do your research, you'll often find that the successful companies have a relatively wide footprint. It's more than just soda with that company.

But never buy stocks, just because a famous investor does. It can just give you an idea where to start. Remember the best idea is just find a solid company.

FINAL WORDS OF FINANCIAL ADVICE

Finally, let me wrap this up by saying that modest gains in your investment portfolio can lead to a great life and comfortable retirement. It just requires the common sense of personal finance that everyone knows. Live below your means, track your spending, pay yourself first, and increase your income streams.

The other obvious headwind to investment gains is debt — credit cards, student loans, medical debt, and your mortgage. There are various schools of thought with this, but I can tell you that most of our significant gains in having a solid comfortable financial footing came after we paid off our credit card, student loan, and auto loan debts.

Now we run a monthly credit card as a cash management tool — with 5% cash back — and pay it off each month. The only debt we have at this point is our mortgage an we have accumulated savings and emergency funds to pay off several months of that mortgage if our finances change.

It took time to get there, and we still made mistakes with money, but we kept at it, and now we're in a much more solid position for long-term growth.

If you're worried about debt, or bad money habits, spend as much time as you can tracking your spending down to the penny. Do this for at least a solid month and you'll be very surprised.

Maybe it's a cliche, but let's talk about those dreaded coffee shops! I love them too... The vibe, the people watching, the great smell of fresh beverages and baked goods, and a cool place to work on the laptop. (By the way, even though it sounds like it based on that description, none of this current project was written in a coffee shop with my headphones on! I wrote this at home in our den.)

A tall coffee frappuccino at your neighborhood Starbucks [ticker symbol: SBUX] might set you back $3.25. Make a habit of that Monday through Friday all month and you're talking $65 a month (5 days a week, 4 weeks a month), and that's without the croissant.

If one share of Kraft Heinz Company is trading at $81.63 and it pays $2.50 per share in annual dividends, it might be nice to know that you could afford to build a position in something like that if you check your spending.

What does future you want you to do? Think ahead, or sip a frappuccino? Even SBUX stock is only $58.76 a share recently and pays a 2.09% yield. The same coffee drink could be a dozen shares a year of Starbucks stock without even trying.

I'm not saying that you shouldn't enjoy your life and your hard-earned money, but it's often the same people complaining that they have no money to start building a nest egg for the future who eat out at restaurants a few times per month and carry it as a balance on a credit card. (My sister who I mentioned before spent so much time spending beyond her means that her credit card debt got out of control years ago. But when she got some finance counseling and debt relief help, they found that her debt was largely gas for her car, dog food, and restaurant charges on her credit cards where she was only paying the minimum.

As I wondered many times before, who wants to pay the premium of credit card borrower's interest on a bag of dog food? Not me, and when she finally understood how silly that was, not my sister either.

Finally, sometimes it's not a debt problem, or spending problem, or bad habits, it's the other end of the spectrum. It's an income problem. It's entirely possible that your entire life and your finances would open up completely and you'd be able to save, invest, and build to your future if you just made a little more each week, a little more each month.

For some this means looking for a better job, asking for a raise, or retraining to enter a different field. For others it means moonlighting, side hustles, and other ways to create a secondary revenue stream.

A friend of mine had all of these grand plans, a great house with a very big mortgage payment, and an employment dream that wasn't brining him enough income each year to feel comfortable.

He was stressed. His wife was very stressed. His whole family felt the weight of every bill that came in. But after a few years of waiting to get paid more (or at least better) in his current situation, he finally opened up some other avenues to make money.

My friend wasn't actually working that much harder in this new chapter of his life, but he was a lot more relaxed, and at the end of the day, he and his wife were a lot happier. (It's why financial expert Dave Ramsey calls his whole world Financial Peace, because that's what comes with better finances: Peace!)

The point of that story wasn't that he was lazy and underemployed and not motivated enough to seek more income. Instead, he was actually trying very hard to make a decent wage from a line of work that was under-appreciated in his area. Yes, perhaps he was stubborn to hold out for so long, but it was only in desperation to make more money each month that he actually took a good hard look at his skills and found other ways to make money without a great deal more effort.

There are new opportunities all the time (the

web economy is a great example), and there are new ways to monetize existing skills and content popping up all the time. Maybe all of your initial investment funds can be generated by money you earn as a side hustle to your main job — maybe as web guru Gary Vaynerchuk always says — in those magical hours between 9pm and 2am, after dinner and when the kids have gone to bed!

Just be patient with yourself, be deliberate in your approach, and always make the effort to understand everything that you are investing in. That has been my guiding principle right from the beginning.

Thanks again for reading this short book and I wish you all the best with your financial journey. Keep learning as much as you can on your path to wealth building.

ABOUT THE AUTHOR

Alan Kerrman is an author and educator from New England who writes about personal finance — among other things — and runs a small, family-owned media company. He has written books about DRIPs (dividend reinvestment plans), a small business launch book, a primer on trading options on technology stocks, and more. He currently invests long-term in dividend paying stocks, and in mutual funds through his workplace retirement account. On his own, he trades stocks, options, futures, and forex in his own self-directed account. (He has also recently dabbled in cryptocurrencies like Bitcoin and Ethereum, but those are not a focus of his long-term investing!) He's not a finance pro, but just an individual investor and trader who is taking charge of his money and wants to share things he has learned along the way. His latest books are available in ebook, paperback, and now audiobook format. Alan Kerrman lives outside of Boston, Massachusetts, USA with his wife and daughter. He runs the site: dripinvestingplans DOT com.

ALSO BY ALAN KERRMAN

To date, **Notable Media** has released three ebooks titles by Alan Kerrman, also available in paperback editions. His book Investing in ***DRIPs: Using Dividend Reinvestment Plans to Achieve Financial Freedom*** is also available in audiobook format narrated by Dave Garner. He has also designed two ***FOREX Trading Log: Trading Journal for forex, FX, or currency market traders.***

Trading Options on Tech Stocks: Selling Puts & Calls: Real Examples to Generate Consistent Option Income and More

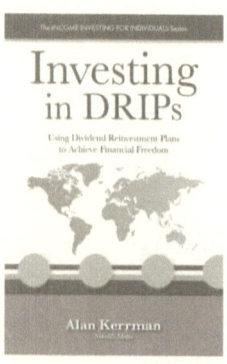

Investing in DRIPs

The Seven Step Rocket Start-Up Plan

Thank you again for reading this and good luck!

AUTHOR'S NOTE

"As I've said before, writing about personal finance, stocks, trading, business, entrepreneurship, and more is a very rewarding process for me. It always has been. I like knowing that people are reading this stuff, learning from the things I've learned and especially from the mistakes I've made. I do think of these author notes as my book 'extras' because you certainly do not have to read them, but if you do you'll get more insight into my overall writing process. This was another fun, rewarding, time-consuming and fascinating book to write, but — as I always say — it feels like it could either be twenty pages or 500 pages long! I want to

keep it short and useful, but there's so much I could cover! I've been blogging and ghostwriting about a lot of this stuff for years, so it's nice to finally publish a few short books sharing my thoughts, approach, and strategies! I continue to learn, want to always provide great value and help others, and I like to add to my growing collection of books and ebooks -- it makes my wifey and daughter proud. (And my daughter has to read them all when she gets older, so that she can know what I know!)

As with other projects of mine in the past, I had this book on pre-order for a little bit before it was published, and I want to now personally THANK those 41 readers (yes, forty-one people), who believed in this project enough to pre-order it. THANK YOU, very much, you know who you are! Your orders, the cure for any possible writer's block, as always kept me motivated!

Lastly, I wanted to say that my books and ebooks are also a part of my own long-

term investment strategy. How? I hope that these books not only help others -- including my family and friends -- but make enough residual sales and royalties over the years to eventually fund my daughter's college plans directly. That would be the perfect scenario: long-term income-based dividend investing, with low fees, paid for by residual royalties from Daddy's time, energy, and writing efforts. Thanks for reading this, and best of luck with your financial world and all of the most important stuff."

-- All best, Alan Kerrman

Please consider leaving a review of this book, and thank you!

INDEX

3D technology, 18
401k, 403(b) account, 10, 34

Alibaba [ticker symbol: BABA], 53
Alphabet [ticker symbol: GOOG], 17, 42, 53
Amazon [ticker symbol: AMZN], 15, 33, 53
Amerian Express [ticker symbol: AXP], 15, 23-25, 27
Apple [ticker symbol: AAPL], 7, 15, 17, 41-42, 53
AquaAmerica [ticker symbol: WTR], 40
auto loan, 58

Bear Stearns, 45
Berkshire Hathaway [ticker symbol: TGT], 56

INDEX

Bitcoin, 2-3, 54
blockchain technology, 2
Buffett, Warren, vii, 6-8, 11, 56

call options, 23-24, 26, 34-36, 38, 40-41, 47, 49, 54-55
cash-secured puts (CSP), 24, 28-30, 37-38, 47
CNBC, 53
Coca-Cola [ticker symbol: KO], 56-57
Computershare, 55
cost basis reduction (CBR), 12-13, 23-24, 27-28, 31, 46
covered calls (options), 34, 47
credit card debt, 58, 60
credit [put] spreads (options), 26, 28, 47
cryptocurrencies, 2-3, 44, 47, 54

Dasani, 57
day trading, 13, 47-48
Disney stock [ticker symbol: DIS], 16, 27-31
diversification, 7, 9, 22, 45, 55
dividend reinvestment plans [DRIPs], vii, 3, 55
dividends, 3, 7, 12-13, 23-24, 26, 28, 33, 35-37, 40-41, 44, 46, 49-50, 52-53, 55-57, 59
DRIPs, vii, 3, 55

INDEX

emergency funds, 58
energy stocks, 21, 55-56
Enron, 45
ETF (exchange traded fund), 44
Ethereum, 2, 54

Facebook [ticker symbol: FB], 45, 53
Fidelity, 53
Fidelity Blue Chip Growth [FBGRX], 53
Finviz, 53
forex (foreign exchange), 47
futures, 10, 47, 54
Fuze, 57

hedging, 12, 44, 54
Honest Tea, 57

index funds, 9-10, 34, 44
inflation, 20

Kraft Heinz Company [ticker symbol: KHZ], 59

margin trading, 30

INDEX

medical debt, 58
Minute Maid, 57
money market funds, 19
Morningstar, 52
mortgage, 58, 61
Motley Fool, 53
mutual funds, 9-10, 32, 44, 52

Nestea, 57
Nestle, 57
non-diversification, 7, 9, 45

penny stocks, 55
Powerade, 57
put options, 23-24, 26-31, 37-39, 47, 49
put spreads (options), 26, 28, 47

Ramsey, Dave, 62
retail apocalypse, 18, 33
retail stocks, 18, 33, 34, 55-56
risk, 2, 9, 18-22, 24, 30, 38, 44
rollover IRA, 25, 33-34, 37
Roth IRA, 32

Samsung [ticker symbol: SSNLF], 21
Sears Holdings [ticker symbol: SHLD], 18
Shareowner Online [Wells Fargo], 55
Sprite, 57
Starbucks [ticker symbol: SBUX], 59-60
stock market crash (1987), 57
student loans, 58
swing trading, 13, 47

Target [ticker symbol: TGT], 25, 33-38, 46, 48
technology, 2-3, 17-18, 22, 55-56
Tesla [ticker symbol: TSLA], 15, 38-40, 53
T. Rowe Price Blue Chip Growth [TRBCX], 52-53
Twitter [ticker symbol: TWTR], 18

utility stocks, 40, 55-56

Vaynerchuk, Gary, 62
virtual reality technology, 18
Vitamin Water, 57

Wall Street, 19
Walmart [ticker symbol: WMT], 16, 45

INDEX

Wells Fargo & Co [ticker symbol: WFC], 7, 15-16, 55

Yahoo [ticker symbol: YHOO], 18, 40, 52
Yahoo Finance, 40, 52